*The Old in Rapallo*

# RORY BRENNAN

**SALMON POETRY**

Published in 1996 by
Salmon Publishing Ltd,
Knockeven, Cliffs of Moher, Co. Clare, Ireland

Copyright © Rory Brennan 1996

Salmon Publishing gratefully acknowledges the
financial assistance of the Arts Council.

The moral right of the author has been asserted.
A catalogue record for this book is available from the British Library.

ISBN 1 897648 82 0 Softcover
ISBN 1 897648 88 X Hardcover

All rights reserved. No part of this publication may be reproduced or transmitted in any form or by any means, electronic or mechanical, including photography, recording, or any information storage or retrieval system, without permission in writing from the publisher. The book is sold subject to the condition that it shall not, by way of trade or otherwise, be lent, resold or otherwise circulated without the publisher's prior consent in any form of binding or cover other than that in which it is published and without a similar condition, including this condition, being imposed on the subsequent purchaser.

Cover painting by O. Brennan
Cover design by Estresso
Set by Siobhán Hutson in Palatino
Printed by Colour Books, Baldoyle Industrial Estate, Dublin 13

*For Orla and Fiona*

## ACKNOWLEDGEMENTS

Acknowledgements are due to the editors of the
following publications in which some of these poems,
or earlier versions of them, previously appeared:
*The Irish Times, The Times Literary Supplement,
Poetry Ireland Review, The Sunday Tribune,
Books Ireland, The Salmon.*

# CONTENTS

| | |
|---|---:|
| The Paper Kisses | 1 |
| The Armada Bell | 2 |
| Feluccas at Aswan | 3 |
| My Mother Paints the House | 5 |
| H Blockages | 6 |
| Rimes | 7 |
| The Wind Messages | 9 |
| Old Negatives | 10 |
| Aeolus Remembers His Random Lovers | 11 |
| The Shellybanks | 12 |
| The Bird Kites | 14 |
| Upstate: Five Day-Trips from New York | |
|     *The Covered Bridges* | 15 |
|     *Primitive School* | 16 |
|     *Field Pieces* | 17 |
|     *The Beaver Dams* | 18 |
|     *The Cellar Holes* | 19 |
| An Alphabet of Death with a Dash of Love | 20 |
| Lines at St. Mullins | 21 |
| The Old in Rapallo | 23 |
| In the Barrel Vault of the North Atlantic | 26 |
| Palladiad | 28 |
| Elsewhere and Clonmacnoise | 30 |
| Timelock | 33 |
| A Child that Didn't Live | 35 |

| | |
|---|---:|
| A Sleeve of Cove | 36 |
| Skin Deep | 38 |
| The Circumcision | 39 |
| Shell Shock | 40 |
| The Turnspit Dog | 41 |
| Putting the Clocks Forward and Putting Them Back | 42 |
| The Crannog at Lisserlough | 44 |
| In the Tsar's Box at the Ballet | 46 |
| John Betjeman in Dublin in the War | 48 |
| Semaphores | 50 |
| The Dot Children | 51 |

## THE PAPER KISSES

A secret invasion of cherubs was what it was like,
This littering of the house with impressions of lips,
Immaculately printed, love's own personal calling cards,
Ghost-mouths whispering inaudible promises,
Ripe beauty hinted in their Cupid's bows.

Pink, mauve, rosé, ochre, vermillion, deep red,
Their shades could match some prism of the moods
Fired by first love's blinkering firework display.
The paper kisses were so perfect as to seem great art,
Fugitive sketches from a Primavera folio.

But they were planted on old bills, junk mail, torn envelopes,
Flyleaves of paperbacks, runic scraps of their father's foolscap,
Mingling with last demands, free offers, blurbs and poems,
Gracing the quotidian with their luscious blooms,
Reminding us we are insubstantial and forgotten
   without love.

Mostly they were to be found near mirrors and telephones
Where hectic lipstickings took place before the dash
To disco, rave, club, bar. Only these last minute dabbings
Were the departure signals of our lovely daughters.
May those who kiss their lips earn their warm hearts.

## THE ARMADA BELL

A belfry is a panoramic shrine.
After the high seas its brass has dulled,
No longer gonging out the watches' time.
The galleon flared out into a bantam line,
Its canvas breast riled up. Then rolled

As it was sprayed with ravelin shot,
Slewed round, a compass in a miscast mould,
One bell-cheeked blast unstoppering the lot.
No cartographer could disguise the blot.
The hull groaned like the keel-hauled, ragged-holed.

The tackle lay along the water line.
O what an afterbirth the sea had foaled!
The hill clansmen took it for a sign
Then took each nail and spar and scrap of twine
To lash the bell to a high pole. They pulled.

The clapper spoke Castilian to the cliffs.
Tardy to hear its syllables unfold
Were the garotted nobles in their ruffs
(Such fopperies spawned spates of belly laughs)
Whose anguish it tolled out. And told.

The curious, like me, make a brief note,
For whom most bells imprison, preach or scold,
Of the neat chapel yard that's now its fate
With the obedient faithful and the late
Sling-hammocked sailors it once called. All cold.

# FELUCCAS AT ASWAN

The Nile is not the colour of eau de nil,
It is more the dregs of a cloudy pale ale brown
As it siphons off so invincibly into the tentacled delta
And the desert sifts in closer to the green-ribbed bank
Like a bedouin drawing his robes about him in the wind
And longing for the original loneliness of the Empty Quarter.

Earlier, up at the ramparts of the High Dam
Two Nubian women spooned off in a coracle to an islet,
Gliding like flies on a mirror in their own reflection
Yet muttering away on some topic, as blithely absorbed
As if everything from Cleopatra to Kitchener had never
    occurred
And another Middle Kingdom pyramid was the latest news.

But the flight from Cairo slid over a neon river,
A cerulean stripe on a daubed canvas of sand,
All in primary colours like a page from a child's Bible,
Till there we were at Aswan and another tiny aircraft
Lay crumpled on the tarmac, wings askew like a swatted moth,
A new hieroglyph for the spun coin of death.

The ghost of Farouk floats through the murky lobby
Of the Old Cataract Hotel, a bloated flounder in an
Ill-kempt fish tank, a shoal of whiteclad lackeys
Minnowing after him. Veneer crinkles on the tables,
Leather chairs are chapped like the palms of fellahin.
No sycophantic nostalgia attends this king.

Parched as bakeries, the tombs tickle the nostril
Into a sneeze. Tutankhamun's virus slips past his smile,
Serene as a script it took millenia to unscramble.
Dust and graverobbers have pre-empted the antiquarians.
I think of secret shafts as I grope down each gallery –
As if death could be appeased by posthumous murder.

Like some law of physics or conundrum of the atom
Where neutrinos and anti-matter frolic and frazzle
The mass and panoply of gods and sacred animals
Just won't repose in the sarcophagus of my skull!
Today you can have the lot, the Liz Taylor statuettes,
The scarabs, the high profile birds, the graffiti-rabid steles.

But in fact it is the model boats and barges
That unmoor my spirit and let the papyrus kiss
Of the past float in on the dune-ferried air –
For who does not long to be borne off to another era,
To have been themselves yet slipped into another life,
To have been themselves unharried by their goads?

So I hire a felucca from one of the tipsters on the front
And slither out to it over boulder and brick-kiln slime,
Then the lateen sail slices down like a guillotine,
Shades the raw sun and decapitates a gust. Off we go,
Out into the heartstream, the great slit artery of Africa,
Till the banks are equidistant and all dilemmas seem
   held at bay.

# MY MOTHER PAINTS THE HOUSE

But what I really mean is that she paints
Pictures of things around the house:
The stained glass apple-green of the hall door,
Its road-lantern red filtering the flow
Of dust-teeming air like traffic lights.
Fruit in a flat ceramic dish she turns into
A laden pleasure barge on a blue cloth
Or makes the giant shipyard crane
Of a three legged stool reshade the floor
Into new territories of light, her charter
Cartridge paper, squeezed tubes and sable hair
To rule with only water. That Hindu festival
Is just her washing line. She paints the stairs –
Light falls across the risers, folds of lace.

## H BLOCKAGES
*for Robert Greacen*

Spies slip up on dialect.
The Great O'Neill used to try out
Tongue twisters on intruders.
One false eclipse,
Then strangled vocal chords
Or a stumble to the block.

The Special Branch sent students
To do Celtic Studies at Queens
So they could tap Gaelic on the telephone
Or interrogate internees.
Is this more urban myth? Like
Asians in attics, coal in baths,
Or Protestants say 'Aitch'
And Catholics 'Haitch'?
The letter in dispute the first
Of *hate, hell, happiness* and
A voice will surely tell us, *hope*.

Spell *holocaust* for us,
Says the man with the gun.

# RIMES

They say it purifies the air,
This white bead curtain of a fall,
As if each droplet were
A lance for a bubonic boil.

But what this dervish veil
For me envelops and unfolds
Are lineaments that still assail,
Things the skeletal weather holds

In abeyance till the chill
Drops its tickertape parade:
From black canyons spill
The sequins of the dead.

I would join up the digit dots
But they won't stay.
Crazy dice are casting lots
Imperturbably.

Under the microscope a flake
Glints like a city from a jet,
A centenarian's birthday cake
Flicking flares at fate.

How small is small? The quark
Scampers through atomic hail,
A missile in the nuclear dark
Of megatons upon its tail.

A micro-universe in pain,
The swirl wraps round a shroud.
A child snowballing again
Lets fling a glass grenade.

The window builds a milky wall.
Cold waits like cossacks in a wood.
They say the snow is general,
Steps stigmatise the road.

The tree wears a lace glove.
Things seem so glazed, alone.
A spent breath of love
Blows frostbite from the bone.

## THE WIND MESSAGES

*In Memory of Anne Kirwan*

Dear Anne, from a seawrack of memories, just two:
First, a sun-kindled bay and a small yellow boat,
A sudden offshore gust had carried you far out ...
That time the ploys of nature did no harm
And you sailed back with sixteen years of life,
And life, exuberantly, was always what you gave.
But in that frail inflatable death dropped a lethal hint.
Next, the summer of eighty-five. You left our house
High on its hill as a brief southern sunset fell
And walked, laughing with friends, down the long slope.
Then far below, by some ventriloquism of the wind,
Through a gap in a toppling dry-stone wall,
Your voice was snatched and swept back up the hill,
Like a bird bearing a message of love in its beak.
Now you are forever out of earshot and a flash flood
Has swallowed up your brain and uprooted all our lives.
Yet above the deluge we still hear your voice. Dear Anne.

## OLD NEGATIVES

With a set of jeweller's screwdrivers
I seek the snagged sprocket, lever, cog,
That will not match or mesh
In this pre-war German camera.

Its back lies open like a small slit trench.
I feel I should squint into an eyepiece
And skulk on the fifth floor of a tenement,
Bent double in the heart of the ghetto.

I twiddle the tiny screws and disinter
Washers and springs. In the summer of thirty-nine
They leapt to order before baroque facades,
Poised fetlocks, Frederick's flourished sword.

Now squares and statues are vague as exposed film
That will never bleach and curl in pasted albums.
A young woman smiled and came home to marry.
So many cameras were less steadily aimed.

No go! It's botched for good, a remnant of its world.
But there's more than a speck of dust in its glaucous lens.
Though made of metal, leather, bakelite and glass
This relic still hoards sediment of splintered bone.

## AEOLUS REMEMBERS HIS RANDOM LOVERS

A dark dense silence declared her rage,
The air was cordite, mist was rifle smoke.
(Calamity Jane on the Deadwood stage.)
*Tina* made forests splinter when she spoke.

Circles on dials and blots on screens,
That's what they tried to make *Marilyn* into.
But she knew how to treat machines,
Smashed them from Mobile to Maracaibo.

*Ellie* had a yen for life afloat
And loved the white-thonged equine manes.
But if you ranged out in your trim-rigged boat
She lashed your hull with the horses' reins.

A sensible sort you might think she was, *Sheila*,
With buttoned-up bodice and thick-soled shoes.
But when she broke out on the tear in Manila
Islands got trampled under her toes.

At the Four Winds Bar in old Brobdingnag
Aeolus knocked back his fiery tequila.
On lonelyhearts nights he'd loosen his bag:
*Tina, Marilyn, Ellie, Sheila.*

## THE SHELLYBANKS
*for Ulick O'Connor*

Long distance trucks have shaken the genteel terraces
For far too long, lugging their deep-frozen innards
Towards Hamburg or Milan past neat bow windows
Where brass telescopes once traced the horizon's
Receding hairline for a tuft of sail. On past
The smart new housing for the unemployed the diesels
Churn and hiss, trailing a dragon tang out to
The crane-forested docks and the ferry's leviathan jaw.

Needing a shield of silence I stride the beach,
Its lined brow gathered at the crowsfeet of pools,
And make for a fringe of tide, the limbs of the bay
Braced to bear the shifting ballast of the city.
Steps squelch in the coiled moulds of worms
I once mined for bait when what preoccupied
Was more innocuous. Far back a heap of bikes
Memorials boyhood like a maritime mark.

Reclaimed land – the very metaphor of memory.
Once all this was something, somewhere else.
The chemical mix of a million households
Is alive to its trove of trinkets and tokens –
 Loveletter, prayerbook, photograph, toy, doll, sketch –
Interred like a ring for luck, a key for a prisoner.
What spells ferment under this skim of earth?
The unsettled ground refuses to rest in peace.

I catch myself glancing round yet again at the town
That exerts some tidal pull on the sargasso weed
That tangles the heart's arteries – or draws it on the rocks.
What stirs in the dark folds of the cauldron of currents?
Love and delight are swept in and out on the ribbed sand
And love's truces are sanctioned in the clasp of hills,
From the slumbering shoulder of Howth to the blunt nipple
Of the Martello tower on the fallen breast of Dalkey Island.

I need no wind at my back to hurry me on,
On towards the spur of beach and the granite ashlars
Of the breakwater, its slabs locking like giant vertebrae,
An uprisen Cyclopean road faring out to the lighthouse.
Here are the Shellybanks and here there are still shells –
Fans, blades, scallops, razors – flecked and spilt
Like sodden confetti in an apse of sand,
Under the scrollwork and tracery of the sky.

Out on the seawall there are gusts and cuffs,
Two centuries of the waves' swell have curved its spine.
On one side the surface is all shot silk,
The other a rag rug.  Nightfall footpads the pier.
Here is the aloneness before homecomings,
Moments when the self is braced once more
For the brunt of love and its broken turnings.
The lighthouse wraps its scarf around the shore.

## THE BIRD KITES

This morning in Beijing we trekked across
The vast red-bannered famous square, a pre-cast Asian steppe,
To see the tiny plastic-doll-pink Mao
Plump as a piglet in his glazed-in trough.
Then off to be processed in the Great Hall of the People
That stank like an old cinema of plush and rexine.

We needed air. The sky was an alloy colander,
Leaking steam. High in the haze at first one speck
Then two and then a whole hovering squadron
Was inspecting us as if we were an infected herd
On the point of keeling over to perish as carrion.
Until at last I saw the spools of the kite-men

Unreeling their paper birds far above the Forbidden City
And felt sheltered, not menaced, by the high hunched flock –
And was at once wound back to towing frail contraptions
Into blustery chill air along childhood beaches,
Trailing down dunes and willing with whoops
The pig-tailed follies to soar and plane like gulls.

A few times they did. Mostly they rose like rocketry,
Then flapped and stalled, looped once or twice – and plummeted.
So it took today in Tianamen Square to teach me
That soft days after all are best for fragile wings,
That kites will rise as effortlessly as prayers
Even if both always have strings attached.

# UPSTATE: FIVE DAY-TRIPS FROM NEW YORK

*for Doug Price and Ellie Stromberg*

*The Covered Bridges*

Round-shouldered Buicks, maiden aunt Model Ts
Play at charades with haycart chaperons,
Their audience an umbrella grove of trees,
The low water chortling over turtle-stones.
Take a stroll down this truncated mine,
Stand in its covering, absorb the shade
Right at the fulcrum, on the river's spine,
Feel how refreshingly your life is weighed
Between two windowscapes of leaf.
Once lovers found a wind-proof shelter here,
Who with the leaves' long furling too have gone,
Tyres thrumming the far murmur of their pleasure.
Where many have passed we can feel most alone –
For what shelter does not retain some grief?

*Primitive School*

Lack of perspective makes their faces flat,
Depth and shadow read from the pulpit of their lives.
It seems they scrubbed their skin before they sat
Stiff in starched white linen by their wives.
The painter made them who they felt they were,
Dotted the children in like pots of flowers,
Delivered the plain masks they'd asked him for.
The light they live in now is purely ours,
Sluiced to our eyes in the bright galleries,
And now their story, like trite fiction, tells
A version too unperturbed to be upheld,
Too like the puritan's plain-wrapper pack of lies
To make us cede the verities of their world.
Only the varnished fissures hint their souls.

*Field Pieces*

Sunglasses serve as filters for a Brady print
Of unstormed slopes.  Fields rise to a palisade
Of stake-thin trees, spectres of a famished regiment.
When stubble cracks their scattered volleys fade.
More evidence: the muzzle-shafts of reapers,
Carts and rakes stick out from long-spoked wheels
And each one dreams a dark blue vigil-keeper
With tilted forage cap, big boots, flare-butted rifle
To guard what seems so strangely little changed.
Why do we so often feel to have come home
In places that are empty and not ours?
These acres have not run wild or gently aged.
Call it the spirit's stand-at-ease, a lifted curse
Gripped in the claws of the rusty reaper's comb.

*The Beaver Dams*

If we humans made this mess we'd be had up
Before the courts, clapped for a breach-of-the-peace in jail.
Since it's a wild animal no one cries stop.
That farmer and his father both peppered them to hell.
Strategist, topographer, the beaver scouts and plots
The contours of his land. The water floods
With the torrential rainfall all the rills and slits
Where every burrowing being scrapes and hides,
Until the last anthill Atlantis is engulfed in dirt.
Then there's the lodge, that odd edifice between
A bulldozed hut in a ghost shanty town
And a swamp house on stilts. Walking we skirt
The dam's tawny edge, its grass all yellow-green,
Knowing the real mess of things is all our own.

*The Cellar Holes*

Frond-bearded traps that lie in wait
For prowlers in the dragging undergrowth
That flanks the car-wide lanes with a low moat.
Missile mosquitoes and cream biplane moths
Dogfight and dive about the open wound,
A trepanned skull of earth, a shadowed pit,
The socket that once locked a house to land.
Of what was here, this is the end of it.
So stand a second at the loose-lipped grave
And hear the tape of anger, laughter, pain,
Run in low volume at top rewind speed,
A race of effort with a purr of love,
Over this half-healed gash the same refrain –
The hiss of time holding his easy lead.

## AN ALPHABET OF DEATH
## WITH A DASH OF LOVE

A is for the Apse where the corpse lies so cold
To B is the verb that no longer applies
C is a Charnel house seeping with mould
D is the shape of those buttoned-Down eyes
E is the Energy drained from your frame
F has to be Fuck, the best one of your life
G is the glorious, execrable Game
And the Goalpost is H where the game came to grief
I am the self, the ego, not others, just me
That J has fish-hooked like Jesus or God
So that K is for Kierkegaard, the soul's referee
Yes, L is for Love, lithe, lustful and languid
That M marries and harries with Murder and Madness
N is the Noose that lolls from the gibbet
And O is the Orifice of earth or of Venus
P preens like Pride and tumbles right in it
Tripped by Q's tail curled like a trick Question
So R ums and eRRs till all forget why
Snakelike Slim S has its slithery motion
T tops off Time, claps the lid on I
U are the other, the only, the one, the Uplifter
That vindictive, vituperative, Viperous V
Will double with W to Waltz out of kilter
X is for Xanadu and the toppled cross-tree
Y is the Yearning sighed with your last breath
Z ends in D and D is for Death.

# LINES AT ST. MULLINS

*for Elisabeth Coyle*

## 1. Lines

Are we reeled in by the barbed spool we cast?
The fantailed leap is like the plunge of bait.
The Barrow here is broad, the seaflow fast.
Dusters of cloud wipe clean the river's slate.

## 2. Tower

The base of the round tower is a rimmed well,
Long silted up and groined with shards and bones.
No flipped coin can crack the mirror's spell –
So spin one up instead among the toppled stones.

## 3. Bell

The bell is shouldered on a beam slung in an arch.
Its rope slacks down, tempts you to twitch or haul
To set the clapper pealing and reclaim the church,
All raftered and reglazed, with plainsong in the aisle.

## 4. Motte

The motte is a huge Norman helmet mad with greed
For furrows to be turned like skirts of petticoat.
Earth-lust; this is its pregnant belly and its seed,
Arms beaten into ploughshares, lands robed in
    chainmail wheat.

## 5. Postcard

This sketch, drawn and printed by John O'Leary, Graigue,
Shows a congregation who risked their necks to kneel.
After such unbowed faith it seems treachery to renege.
Only the priest and the look-out have their backs to the people.

## 6. Church

The last church here is a local landowner's one,
Rendered cement among rain-laundered Romanesque
But weathered enough to match mason-crafted stone,
One more artefact for Christ's unacted masque.

## 7. Stones

The tombstones jostle, lean and slump like men
Who've run a course and can't gulp back their breath.
In bold or in italic, ten slabs decipher Brennan
Over two centuries. This site is old. They only camp in death.

## THE OLD IN RAPALLO

The sea has aged skin, is restless like the old.
There is a flood along this esplanade
Where the cast-iron knotted wood has sores
That seep through wrinkles in the pale white paint,
Thin limbs blotted with the bruise of rust.
I lean against a railing, take in how the sea
Fritters away its force, loses its grip on weed.
Only the beggars are younger than me here.

Now at forty I share scraps of the century
And trespass across eighty-five odd years
As I slip into the clogged procession
That flows both ways at once and so stays
A sluggish river. All afternoon the elderly
Trundle or shuffle, traverse the promenade,
One broad stream without an estuary
Above the loose-gloved, ill-sewn sea.

They all have known what I sought to imagine,
The sickled dates that lopped and culled the world –
But now I feel I know that selfsame heavy map.
From the crater over my breastbone to the knoll
Of my ankle a livid trenchwork travels,
Only skirting the salient of my genitalia.
Self-cannibalized, transplanted arteries supply
My refortified, Verdun-assaulted heart!

I have slipped back under the coiled wire,
Gulp with delight clear draughts of air. Along
The flowerbeds a young gipsy simpers for coins,
An African offers fake ivory. I also deal in supine pace
And posture, a convalescent, transient in the swirl
That's a limbo mezzotint, a doom-tract throwaway,
A scrap of Ezra's prattle as he slung chicken bones
At wasp-eyed cats. When all the old were young.

In her draped cheeks I see my lover's flush,
In a drawn waist another arching back.
The blur and trace of beauty keep their own counsel,
Brave the corniche and dare their memories,
Group, dawdle and disband as if this masque
Were the parody and fate of all relationships.
The onshore air is warm with scents of flesh,
Rocks lick their fingers on the sweetish spray.

In this resort of treaties and irascible poets
The old are so polite, so tremulously suave,
It seems tactic and ploy have trumped the fiery word,
Urbane diplomacy doused Yeatsian ire.
Until in the gorge of the hills the thunder
Clears its throat like the heckle of dead dictators,
For poets and public men both courted disaster –
What quotes won sly approval, prompted gold-plated pens?

The old inhabit the dripping canopy of death.
I've strolled inside their cavern and been plucked
From the turned tide by a kind scalpel blade
Falling like a needle of sheer light. Soon dark
Will tumble the hipped mountain on the town,
A haze of decades mist its balustrades.
Then the throng will thin to footloose streaks
Loitering under arc lamps like the years.

## IN THE BARREL VAULT
## OF THE NORTH ATLANTIC

Ice makes tracing paper maps along the wing,
Pop rivets pimple cowlings. The turbine's jaw
Hangs slack and open like a landed trout's.
Away below a stippled mesh shows where

The sea has strained in the net-casts of night.
Past all catnapping now, I've lost the traveller's sense
Of refuelled purpose, of one more start, of a dead skin shed.
The riddling on the nerves' fraught harness keeps in tune

With the aileron whose friction rubs a bar of light
In a pale arc around a stonecut cupola,
A dawn some fasting penitent might once have seen
In a cold chapel before a test of faith.

A mosquito in Mercator's bellied web
We shiver at three hundred miles an hour,
A frisson faster (so it seems) than those asleep can feel,
Not waiting for the pink-tipped tongs of glare.

Small jugglers' clubs, digital numerals tumble
And do their sleight of hand. With a ballpen
I tap a present of five hours into my daughter's watch,
Wondering where on earth she'll choose to cash them in,

As if time's three-card-trick was not simply ourselves,
Gladfingering soiled notes, loose change and foreign coins.
The sun's long fuse has flared. We fly on into it again,
Grateful like old wheel-jolted passengers for a re-coopered rim.

# PALLADIAD

Behind the plaster and the lath
The woodlouse pioneers his path.

The weight inside the window sash
Waits for a puff of wind to crash.

The cornice and the architrave
No arts society can save.

Like a bent finger the chimney sags,
Beckoning the butler who packed his bags.

The bellpull cannot summon the parlourmaid.
It cannot ring to wake the dead.

Wildflowers and weeds dispute the lawn
Where duellists flung the gauntlet down.

Through the bedroom window a branch sticks its head
Where the abducted bride was brought to bed.

Here comes the crane and the wrecker's ball
For the portico, the dome and the stone-flagged hall.

Now what will they build here? A flash hotel
That will mimic the old proportions well,

With squash, jacuzzi, nouvelle cuisine
To exorcise the ghosts of the *ancien régime*.

What's going up is as easy to scorn
As what went before is hard to mourn.

# ELSEWHERE AND CLONMACNOISE

*In Memory of Conleth Ellis*

Like all the cherished dead you are always with us
And will never abscond, though our grief might wish it.
Only with other deaths will you shyly quit the world
And even then your poems like cloud and river
Will exchange their elaborate evening secrets.
Sunset, all too surely, was your time of day.

But your own cherishing heart is all too dead
And we are appalled it is erased as utterly
As the myriad interlacings of so much memory
Or that vista of sudden rapture we call imagination.
Your arteries had no right to silt up and garotte
A bloodstream driven by such generous beats.

Classroom, rostrum, desk – the screech of chalk
Howls across thirty years. You stand at the blackboard.
Grey-suited and far too young to be enlisted again
In the siegeplan of schools. Branches flexed at the window.
Leonardo might have sketched or Mozart played
To small avail with us. But I hear you holding forth.

The Rathmines Road in nineteen fifty-nine,
All Ireland a faded postcard! But definition returned
Beamed to a larger screen, old teacher became firm friend
When long later the identikit clicked in your rueful smile.
What sidesteps us into the steep impasse of words?
In your obituary I wrote, *he taught three poets*.

Down a pilgrimage road straight as a saint's staff
We once drove towards Clonmacnoise, our tyres
Outracing the trudge of centuries, your talk lightly
Treading in Latin and Irish. With finest scholars from –
Let's pick and choose – Iona, Antioch, Kiev,
You'd hold a fair debate and hold your own.

But you had to learn the stunning inadequacy of brilliance,
So savage since the truth came shining from your hands,
And had to watch, like someone stumbling into a bad play,
The slick win a round of death-rattle applause,
The talentless pander and tout for the driest grain
Of praise or notice. Such famine relief you refused.

The country schoolmaster with integrity! How well
You came to recognise the lies of your own land,
What lay behind the hillocks in cultivated landscapes.
You trusted us to know our trade and were wrong.
How many less intent souls would have called it a day?
Slowly your books came to light like unearthed texts.

At your funeral I could picture you starting to smile,
Arms folded across your chest, half-glancing down,
Leaning against a pillar, a mild sardonic grin
Puckering your lips at the tiring orotundities
Of these uncanny proceedings, honing a barb of wit.
But death is a poor hand at jokes against himself.

When you flew in a small plane over Serengeti
The years must have seemed like fleeing antelope,
Way back to the evenings of hard-earned early poems
When bells had clanged and schoolyards eddied out.
If I have lost your postcard from Mombasa I have kept
Like title deeds the trust you stored in words.

Now you are borne to mind in a saga of elsewheres
But most of all in the chancel at Clonmacnoise,
The late sun hoisting its slashed pennant on the water
As if waiting for the shields of a Norse longboat
To ignite a slain skald's pyre. Elsewhere and always,
By and beyond river and ruined arch, so you remain.

## TIMELOCK

The key left outside on a sill
Has leaked the circles of its clover leaf.
The locks are changed. It never will
Turn round again and grind its teeth.

It has left its impression
In rose-madder rust instead of ink,
A signet set into the stone.
I pick it up once more and think

Of those that it let in and out.
And how once the locksmith's art
Was mundane but still elaborate –
Things cast to play their part.

Children, their eyes just key-hole high,
Peered through the minaret of dark
And aged like Alice suddenly
With an adult's chance remark.

Late-nighters eased the spring around
And tiptoed up the stairs.
The clicks and creaks made the same sound
Parents listened for for years,

Since the tradesman sank the deadlock in
And lined the receiver up.
Can the world continue on its spin
If the tumblers of memory stop?

Now I make a monocle from the key
Or a magnifying glass,
But a vacant garden is all I see,
Not picnics on the grass.

Old house, I pull your door again.
I am the last; we've had our day.
The sun will bleach, the rain
Will wash imprints and family away.

There is far too much for us to save.
I toss the key into a flower-bed,
No fitter end for odds of love
And all the land-locked dead.

# A CHILD THAT DIDN'T LIVE

*for Dorothy and Don*

So many came to the chapel in the maternity hospital
That we were standing packed together on the winding
    staircase
Like refugees queueing in vain for a visa to a country
That didn't exist but yet we were trying to reach.

The death of an infant is a windblown spark too rapid to
    be seen.
Life craves a span of light; we can only suffer so much dark.
When you both came out of the morgue with that small
    white coffin,
The size of a tradesman's toolbox or a weekend case

And placed it in the back seat of your car and got in
And drove off with it there behind you – your bravery
Drew all our love after you in the longest cortège,
Far beyond the high-walled cemetery and the tiny
    unsealable tomb.

# A SLEEVE OF COVE

A sleeve of cove, the sea frayed herringbone,
With upturned boats rebuttoning its cuff,
And then right there, under the collar of the hill,
The pectoral muscle, a pocket-patch of church.

A mandala of capitol, a marble column cap,
Sunk into the wall above the door,
Its ring of flowers clinging like wet lace,
Marks how the antique lay anchored in Byzantium.

On such a sacred spot, the open secrets say,
Dionysians emptied amphoras of unwatered wine,
The beach coiled with lovers like Medusa's hair,
And followers of Mithras sought the temple's shade.

Still here at night the routine seems the same,
The screech of two-strokes in ritual agony,
Rock music thumping the taut drumskin of lust.
Only in the afternoon, the tiny church and peace.

There are a thousand more along these shores,
Linked out like worry beads, all seagull-white,
That from the sea seem totems, bleaching skulls.
And each cranium contains what is found here:

A branching candelabra for tapers of honey wax,
A tin for alms, a screen of flimsy wood for saints
To strike less posing attitudes than in basilicas.
So I will leave a few rolled-up notes, at least

A drachma for each year the church has stood.
Lost far below lie small child's-circle coins,
The ruler's profile more engrained with dirt
Than the last worshipper's sign-crossed palm.

## SKIN DEEP

The skinhead sycamore seems set to bud.
Last year two agile tinkers scaled
Its horny back, lopped off its sixties locks
And scalped its tousled hair. It stood
All winter like a prop from Lear
On the dark stage of my garden
Till spring showed up its adolescent spots,
Then it sprouted twigs, straight as six-inch nails.
They said it was traumatised by its chainsaw
Dismembering. Now it refoliates, a small canyon away
From my granite sill. We both boast hidden scars.

## THE CIRCUMCISION
*Morocco 1969*

The family had fetched a rabbi as old as Moses
In from a village in the Middle Atlas to do the job.
He was well grounded in Talmudic commentary –
    if shaky on his feet.
What if the blade slipped in his twiglike fingers?

He bent over the cradle and the baby pierced the air
With a shriek like a faulty horn on a Tangier taxi.
There was no mishap. The aged rabbi turned round and
    smiled
And everyone clapped, slapped backs and laughed and
    sipped

The dark sweet wine and munched dry pastry cakes.
I thought of the forty or so medieval monasteries
That laid claim to the unresurrected foreskin of Christ.
*That boy's a few ounces lighter now*, the father said.

## SHELL SHOCK

Scoop your palm to the whorls of your ear,
Slip the soft clams over your eyeballs.

It's like standing still at the mouth of a tunnel
And hearing the air inhaled by the draught,

Only it really is blood irrigating your veins
Far out into the ox-bows of your lobes.

Still, that cannot suffice. Nor will it do to say
It is some fabricated acoustic, a mage's subterfuge,

The way a guide crumples paper or strikes a match
At the altar site in a classical theatre

And the crunch or scratch is syllabically clear
Above the chatter of tourists and the brushing of the pines

Even as far up as the back of the topmost tier.
So tilt your head and tune the pitch of your eardrums:

The sound rises and falls like the cheers of a crowd
At a sports meeting half a dozen fields away.

Keep on listening until with a roar it brutally dawns:
It can only be the future fleeing the abominable past –

Who could doubt it who knows the noise of our century?
And all of us seed-dust spilt and torn in the spiral.

# THE TURNSPIT DOG

His tail bobs to the beat of a whisk.
The French chef rips off a sliver of crackling
And tosses it into the trap of his jaws.
Shanks trample, the treadmill turns
Like a cheap act in a travelling circus.

The glistening carcass of an impaled boar
Shifts round and round above its lava bed,
Spattering the coals with exploding globules.
The smell alone would nourish a village,
Like the one transplanted for the Italian park.

Upstairs the footmen stand in line
Like some old commedia dell'arte chorus.
Back down below in the raucous kitchen
Scullions chop, strain, baste, stuff, curse

And the mongrel shits inside his tripping wheel.
A menial is yelled at to tidy the mess
Who returns sharply but unscrubbed from the pails
To sprinkle nutmeg on the lemon mousse.

## PUTTING THE CLOCKS FORWARD
## AND PUTTING THEM BACK

Once a whole century idled between each swivel,
The minute hand deriding the hour's cavil.

The winter six were the tundra's long reach,
Summer's half dozen a stretch of beach.

O Time and Space, the slow motion globe
Was the Song of Solomon and the Book of Job.

Life seemed as long as a rice-paper Bible.
Now it's down to the merest slim vol.

And the face on the dial has started to spin;
The curve of time is the clock's blurred grin.

Was it only last week that I moved it on?
To turn it back will yield no gain.

Not hearing the gunshot is what it's like.
You're around if you notice midnight strike.

Wind the spring to the last choked click;
At the bar of time there's no free tick.

Just leave it to a microchip of quartz
To squeeze a lifespan till it hurts.

The months of winter are a wet afternoon,
Those of summer a stab of sun.

# THE CRANNOG AT LISSERLOUGH
*for Paul McLaughlin Hyde*

The lake displays its levels like an unscoured bath;
Scum, human or mineral, is as grey as truth.
But at least history is not blank between the watermarks,

Low and high are littered with spent shells –
Crustacean ones, not old artillery rounds –
Though they are cloudy white as bones at Gallipoli

Or even Troy, just up the road in time from our crannog,
That skulks offshore like a scraggy plume on a tin helmet,
Headbutting the wind, a roughneck refusing to answer
    questions.

It still upholds its little pride of place, right here
And as a coded tick on an archaeologist's plan
Rolled up in the oubliette of a department archive,

Or glinting on a PC screen, not quite the way it does
When rain, moonlight and shadow adjust their radar
And the lake transfers on to another kind of disc.

The crannog has endured the arc from slingshot to missile,
Annotated along the way by a naval cartographer
Who swung the lead and scoped the shore for croppies.

So it is just a bit more than merely itself
Or a talking point for us as we stroll the knobbly beach.
We pat the rump of an upturned rowing boat

And sit on it uneasily as if waves were underneath,
Not fist-sized stones. But the crannog is too ungainly and too old,
A smarting penknife-notch still on the soul.

Away in the trellis of trees are a few lozenges of rouge:
A professor from Italy is restoring a hunting lodge.
A splash of the Veneto has alighted in Leitrim

And is more than welcome. Roscommon and Sligo too
Wear their crannogs like crowns of thorns at their heart
And frame them with spare and brittle breastworks.

We head back on the scent of steaming whiskeys,
Leaving those drizzly midgets on their clod and wicker islets
To itch in their noxious skins around a consumptive fire.

# IN THE TSAR'S BOX AT THE BALLET

The exquisite ballerina told us,
You know the KGB men by their ugly wives!
(There is not that strain of political correctness in Russia –
Theirs is monitored in watchtower signs on maps.)
But what she said was true – not that the men were
    handsome:
Stone-bald, tent-suited, sandpaper-jowled,
With eyes deep-set and dark as empty cartridges,
There they sat in the tsar's old opera box,
Waiting aggressively to be ridiculed by Bond,
Ghost-thugs from *Dr No* knouted by glasnost.
And yes, their wives were very much the same
(Fleming would have made much of their moustaches)
Only they were decked out in red curtain material
Or perhaps some off-the-lorry stuff for flags
Which still rippled in floodlights over the Kremlin
And a Red Square angst-ridden for the kettledrum of tanks.
Towing us like freed serfs past bankrupt boyars,
The superb dancer flounced into the tsar's enclave.
The apparatchiks gave us small sour helpless smiles –
So that's the way, I thought, these regimes end,
Not with a clang but a simper. Well Stalin's name
Was also a pun, nor does it make him less brutal.
Did Rasputin despoil young princesses in here?
(Oh the ballet tended to toe – à point! – the party line:
Men in riding boots, girls in embroidered skirts.)

Then our hostess swept us off to the ballroom
Where couples listlessly paraded in circles
Like privileged prisoners trudging out their Siberia
Or exhibits in the ring of a mock-auction history,
Sick to death of being told they are repeating themselves.

## JOHN BETJEMAN IN DUBLIN
## IN THE WAR

Around the square the poet trundles
While Europe lets off all its guns
To a shop where books are piled in bundles,
Jampacked with rhymes, laments and puns,

His arms against iniquity.
From Clare Street and dust-pencilled Greene's
He ambles off through Trinity,
Imbibing deep of Irish scenes:

The storm clouds over College Park
Are neutral as black spears of sleet.
To counteract the wing-droned dark
He takes Bewley's tea in Grafton Street

Where sweet doe-eyed flirtatious creatures
Pout and grin at long-scarfed students.
Encoded signals cross their features,
Enigmatic innocence.

Then he unwraps his latest purchase
Under panes by Harry Clarke,
But in his mind in silver chase
Stamps Ireland with his own hallmark.

A place of cornice, fanlight, stone,
Blessed with Tom Moore and melancholy,
Where great gaunt houses stand alone
Guarding fields of hump-backed hay.

Mad dowagers in Rathmines flats,
Golfers in loud plaid plus-fours,
Wives in herbaceous border hats,
Hell-raisers on the tear,

The squireen and the glowing girl
From peeling Hall and whitewashed farm,
John Betjeman fine-etched them all
While the world yelled out in war alarm.

Let's walk him back to Merrion Square.
(He works in the embassy there as a spy!)
There's a touch of spring in the brightening air,
Less espionage than poetry,

For words, not secrets, was his skill.
He lilted at windmills of truth
And lanced them with a springy foil
That stored the suppleness of youth.

## SEMAPHORES

Winter seasides are woefully sad: here people tried to be happy.
The spray on the pier crash-tackles the lighthouse.
In black-hole arcades bright manic machines twitter and blink.
But who drifting through is not tempted to linger?

Where else would you read the tabloid that wrapped
 your chips?
Where else gobble chips? The days' undoings are
 transparent with grease,
The page-three girl is tattooed with massacres in Bosnia.
One could go on like this till the end of the promenade

And record little new. What lodges is the lawn-bibbed
 yacht club,
The cigar stub of its cannon and its yard-arm semaphore,
Standing there with its wet veranda a storm-tossed taffrail
Waiting for a legendary captain to go down with his ship.

Last summer the flags flapped their signals to the fleet
That raced their white arrows on the trajectory of the sea.
The semaphore has the air of a restless gibbet now,
Right set to swing the local hooligans and the club bore.

And the cannon coughed and blew its smoke-ring – but
What saddens most is all the mad blunders flagged from masts
How admirals hung back and in their turn were hung.
Winter seasides sing like stays and cordage with lost signals.

# THE DOT CHILDREN

The track slips down the hill,
Squiggles and feints a bit,
Just enough to trip a thought
About mazes and thread
And tunnels stripped bare
By stone-mad magnates,
Like that pit in Crete
Only a day's sail
Over the unravelling sea.

But on the flat the path
Flakes it with a few swerves
For hundreds of yards
To cut like a T-square
The new asphalt road
Laid down the valley
In our time here,
Straight as an airstrip
And often as vacant.

Before that the old way was
Rutted as a retreated seabed
That shuddered our motorbikes
Like Poseidon's handshake,
One child on your pillion,
The other on my petrol tank,
We jarred and gurgled home

(Sometimes all four of us
On one swaying machine!)
Over the spine of the island
Under a gold-mask moon
Through the gentle Aegean dark
And into the womb-labyrinth
Of family myth.

When the children took
To their own four feet
They trekked or hitched
Back and forth from
Beach and village.
When a car drew up
Half a mile or so off
We'd see two dots alight
And start along the track,
A tiny pair of commas
On the scalding screen
Of a heat-hazy afternoon
Such as only Greece can kindle.
As if one pressed a cursor
They grew larger – only
It was their own dusty sandals
That drew them closer
Till they were identifiable,
Hand in hand-swinging
Like siblings in fables
Trailing through woodcuts.

Sooner that we'd think
The dot children had landed
Up at the house on the hill
Laughing and yelling,
Thirsting to be cooled down,
Like pots boiling over.

Though the girls have grown
Into gorgeous women
And are far from the island,
Now and then my glance darts
All the way down to that T
Of track and tarred road
And I spy two dots again
But only after I've been
Staring into the blazing sky
And transposed two
Dancing sunspots.